Don't Wait Til I Die to Love Me

Copyright Disclaimer

Michael Tavon

Dear Reader,

I'd like to thank you for
supporting my work and my dreams. I
hope this book inspires you, I hope
this book fulfills you emotionally.
From the bottom of my heart I thank
you for allowing my words to be a
part of your journey.

Don't Wait Til I Die to Love Me

Come as You Are

It's hard to love
With a fragile heart
When the world is made of stone
It's hard to sleep at night
When you're tired of being alone

Come as you are
I need nothing more
Bring your heart
Don't hide the scars

Come as you are
As the friend I truly need
My heart needs your empathy

Like a hollow box
I'm deep
but filled with nothing
The pain of being alone
Can be so numbing

I cling to things
Not good for me
just to feel something
I keep going and going
100 miles and runnin'

Come as you are

Michael Tavon

nothing less

Come as you are
Without the stress

Come as you are
Bring your pain,
And leave the drama
I need you here with me

One Call Away

I was too blind to see

You only wanted me

For the comfort

I provided during

your time of need,

When you got back on your feet

I was left in the rearview

Along with your pain and mistakes

I'm happy you found yourself

It's truly a beautiful thing

But it hurts I have to witness

You shine from afar

Maybe, I was placed

in your life

Michael Tavon

to be there

When you were falling apart

And once you put the pieces

back together,

You felt strong enough

To stand on your own

Thank you for allowing me in during

Your most difficult time

And trusting me to place bandages

On your broken heart

Just know

if you ever need me again

I'm one call away

The Message

Tell the ones you love most

All the kind words

You held your tongue to say

Create new memories

To make up

For all the time lost

Embrace them

like it's your last

time holding them

in your arms

send an uplifting

message to brighten their day

Michael Tavon

small gestures

go a long way

Burn every grudge

Don't let your pride

Be the reason why

You can't apologize

So please,

Be good to those you love

No hour is guaranteed

Because losing someone,

with conflicts unresolved

Words never said,

And messages unread

Is the type of guilt

That will eat you

alive

Eviction Notice II

It's time for you to leave
You've been living
In my mind far too long,
I stored
the memories we shared
In a carry on
So you can carry on
And hit the road,
It's difficult for me
to let you go
But allowing you to
stay on my mind
is killing me more
So please move far away
From my mental space

Michael Tavon

Don't Wait 'til I Die

Don't wait til I die to love me
Wash away my doubts and fears
shower me with praise
While I'm still here

Make my eyes marvel
at the sight
Of the flowers I deserve
Don't wait til I'm in an urn

Please don't wait til I'm gone
to me sing a song
Let me hear your voice
while I can sing along

Please don't wait til my body
Expires to hug me tight

I'll be warm
I promise, I won't bite

Don't hold back
Tell me how you feel
Because 'I love you' means nothing
If I'm not here

Her Story II

Her story is too complex

For the simple minded

to comprehend

So, she keeps her heart closed

Like an antique novel

Hoping one day

someone with a mind so beautiful

Will come along

to give her the freedom

to be vulnerable enough

to open her cover again,

As the dust blows from the

Pages of her past

The phrases and metaphors

Used to detail her intricacies

will be exposed to light

Until then,

Michael Tavon

She remains closed

but hopeful

Keeping her peace

by not allowing simple minds

to have access to her story

because she refuses to be

open, broken, and misunderstood

all over again.

Head rubs

I feel the passion
you have for me
Through the sensation
of your fingertips
When you massage my scalp

Your magic touch
Makes the stress
of my day disappear

As I drift into a daydream
You whisper
'I love you' into my ear,

your traveling lips
Lands on my forehead and neck

Falling asleep to the grace
Of your touch
Mends the chaotic chasms
In my mind

You, caressing my head
Feels like cool rain
after a blazing day

Michael Tavon

Blue Jay

Love should be as natural
To humans
as flying is to a blue jay
Sadly, we let time destroy us
The older we grow
The less love we show
Using our pride as shields
To prevent our hearts from telling
Loved ones how we really feel
Because we're afraid to get broken,
Disappointed
As time goes by
We forget how to love
and slowly turn into stones
I wonder,
Would a blue jay stop flying
After being knocked
down by a few storms?
I doubt it.
So why are we afraid to love
After we get hurt?
Pain should make us
Want to love harder
Not become distant,

Or seek vengeance,

Don't Wait Til I Die to Love Me

the next time
Fear strikes your heart
when you yearn for love
Or your mouth
Glues shut
When you want to tell
Someone how much
they mean to you
Stare at the blue jay in the sky
And think of the storms
It survived
And how it continues to fly
Bold and high,
Love has wings
Never stop flying

Heaven on Earth

How lucky am I
To have found
heaven on earth
Away from darkness,
And cleansed of dirt

How lucky am I
For this space of peace,
where I feel whole,
Where I feel complete.

I've found heaven
While my heart still beats
most don't find until
they're 6 feet deep
Funny,
Heaven was never
Hard to find
For, it was always here
Inside my mind

Beauty Within

look into the mirror; instead of
picking
at your flaws
Smile and remind yourself how
divine you are

Michael Tavon

The Hurricane

Somedays she's

like a calm breeze

bringing peace

on a burning summer day

other days,

she's a hurricane

self-destructing

her own mind.

to love her is to know

if she's there to cool

you down on your hottest days

she deserves someone

who doesn't run

when the weather gets brutal.

remain by her side

to help her pick up

the broken piece

when the storm settles

Stargazer

She prefers a night
of stargazing
as raindrops tap dance
on the window,
over nightclubs
Any day of the week.
Most call her a bore
But I, find nothing more
Exciting than sharing
the moon alone with her

Michael Tavon

<u>Hotter Than July</u>

Your love burns hotter
Than a cloudless July sky
I melt when you stare

Five Senses

Two hands to feel
Two ears to listen
Two nostrils to smell
Two eyes to pay attention
And one tongue between
our cheeks
Only to speak and eat

As humans we're born
with the proper tools to be
empathetic
Loving beings
This earth, was crafted for us
To prosper together

Yet and still
Too many people,
Speak before listening
Speak before observing
Speak before feeling
Speak before learning

The tongue is not meant
to be used as a weapon
It's for asking questions
To gain better understanding

Michael Tavon

Instead, people use
words to curse
To hurt.
destroy,
Hate,
Manipulate.

Why do people act this way?
Refuse to listen but quick to
judge?

People rush to be

loud and wrong
when they lack the patience

to be silent and learn

Golden Rule :

Give her the love
she deserves,
In return you'll discover
A universe within yourself
You never knew existed

Michael Tavon

I Think I Love You

I Fell In love with you
Out of the blue,
Too soon
It seems
You've erased the blues
From my weary heart
Now it beats in hues bright enough
To Carry through the darkest
depths of the ocean
I'm open,
Hoping
This feeling
Feels new forever

Loneliness,

Feels like hearing echoes
In a crowded room
Or More like feeling nothing while
Fucking someone who has no love for
you
To feel lonely is to feel worthless
Like your existence serves no
purpose
You fall down this dark hole
Of feeling neglected
From the world,
You become restless
And dejected
You wonder if anyone would hear
If you cried for help

loneliness is really
The lack of love for self
See, when you admire your
solidarity
And find comfort in being alone
Your mind becomes a home
Of peace
You'll find it easier to breathe
Between the empty spaces
You won't yearn for company
Again,
When you become
Your own best friend
where to begin

Michael Tavon

This journey is the hard part
It's a battle long fought

Some days will be a storm,
You'll get caught in
But when you fight to survive
You'll feel the sunshine
You'll see the light
Of being alone

The Courage

She isn't afraid
to use her voice
Because it holds
The force of an ocean

Michael Tavon

Starlight
(verse)

I dreamt about you
this morning
Always do when
I'm lonely or loathing
Always on my mental
Even when not meant to
Love is a gun
And you're a sex pistol
For you I'd take a shot
To the chest
I confess I'm obsessed
When I leave a text
I'm never left on read
Make it last forever, Keith sweat
How did I live before you
'cause I only live for you
Baby I adore
More than cordial
You took a lonely heart
And made it so hopeful
My hope is full
You're the starlight
In my dark mind
When I get lost

Don't Wait Til I Die to Love Me

You're not hard to find
Love doesn't hide
It's in plain sight
I thank the sky
You're all mine

Michael Tavon

Power of Words

A celebrity has
the power of fame
The president has the
power of resources
I, a writer,
have the power of words,
Such a tremendous responsibility
For someone so young
I just hope
I'm doing well by the universe

A Letter to the Hearts I Broke

I don't deserve to play victim I've toyed with my fair share of hearts when I was bored or felt lonely. I yo-yo'd with the trust of good women, because I was too cowardly to vocalize my true intentions. So, I could never play victim when Karma paid a visit to collect its debt. I hope the hearts I broke have been restored; I hope they find the love they were hoping for, the love they thought they felt with me. I hope my deceit did not turn them cold. I know they all know, I'm not a bad guy, they just found me at the wrong time. I was

ashamed of who I was, and they
didn't deserve to be misled,
ghosted, or used; because I was a
broken mess looking for someone to
fill the void in my soul. To the
hearts I've broken I hope you're
reading this, I hope you forgive me
or at least understand.

For the Educators

This special little poem is
dedicated to
The teachers,

The childcare workers,
And educators in all fields,
thank you for sacrificing late
nights,
and early mornings. You're
underpaid and overlooked,

 but continue to bust your asses
for the students with class.

You change lives, enlighten minds,
you are the bright spot to a lot of
bleak days.

Keep feeding the young souls who
starve for education.

Michael Tavon

Coming to an End

Society values money

More than love

They treasure diamonds

more than time

and treat earth like a dumpster

As the food we eat

becomes more poisonous

and pollution fills the oceans

I wonder if God

Has anymore tears left or

Any chances to spare?

Has God grown tired

Of saving us

As trees set ablaze,

glaciers melt into puddles,

hurricanes flood cities,

Don't Wait Til I Die to Love Me

and animals vanish.
Are these natural disasters
the beginning of the end?
Is it too late to save us now?
Is it too late to care?

You're not a Bad Person

Sometimes when you're young with a confused heart, and a mind that is spiraling like a tornado you do things you don't mean. You alienate the people who want to hold you close and you break hearts, unintentionally. This does not make you a horrible person. What makes you a terrible person is repeating the same toxic habits and refusing to take accountability for the pain you inflict; or choosing to not grow from your mistakes. If you've broken a heart or two, you're not a bad person. You still have the potential to be a wonderful soul if you continue to learn from the people you hurt.

Speed

The speed of life
is often too fast
for my feet
to keep pace

Michael Tavon

2 the prettiest soul I've ever met,

When you open your heart
In a world of despair
Moons and constellations
Fills the air
Creating a universe of your own
A majestic sight to behold.

A Dream Deferred II

Am I chasing
the impossible dream?
I've been running for years
I feel it my back and knees

Why do I keep going?
What is my motive
To keep running towards
A goal that seems like nowhere

far from where I started
but further from the finish
I'm stuck dead in the middle
Jaded and winded

Do I keep running
Til my final breath
Maybe I don't know.
But giving up
Is worse than death

*inspired by Langston Hughes's What
happens to a dream deferred*

Intelligent Heart

Falling in love with you

Is by far the smartest thing

My heart has ever done

Ode to Childhood

I miss the days
When we were too young
to understand
chaos, pain, and stressing
Before we were hit with taxes
And depression.
So young and carefree
we used to be,
Splashing wildly in the
Knee deep swimming pool.
Doing wheelies
on the silver mongoose,
Dancing on the front lawn
like footloose,

And tossing the pigskin
All afternoon
Summer days
Were filled with adventure,
'Til the streetlights shined
We would scatter like roaches
Rushing back inside
Life was so easy
because we were blind
To the troubles at night.

Funny,
how we couldn't
wait to grow up

Michael Tavon

Now we wish
we could stop getting older

Parents told me
to be careful

what I wish for
I should've listened back then

Track Star

For your love
My heart became a track star
Constantly sprinting
for your affection
And jumping over the hurdles
You placed in front of us

I thought you were
Playing hard to get
By running away
So I continued to chase
The fantasy of you and I

In the end
My efforts fell short
I wasn't good enough
I came dead last
But I can't complain
'Cause of you
My heart is now
In premiere shape

For a love that's willing to last
for me

Michael Tavon

Nostalgia III

We yearn for the days

long gone

We cling to the feelings

brought by memories fading.

We beg father time

To refund two thousand yesterdays

So, we can do it all over again

We attach ourselves to the past

Hoping that joy would come back

Through it all,

We become addicted to these
thoughts

and conjure up misery

by reaching for what we can't touch

Nostalgia,

is one hell of a drug

Ethereal

Those who only
know me externally
Will never understand
the universe
that lies within
this ethereal soul of mine

Hurt You

I apologize for using
Your affection
As a temporary fix
When I was addicted
To feeling loved

I feared being alone
So I used you to fill
The void
Until I found another home
For my misery to dwell

I used my smile to lure you in
I was the nice guy
You should've been warned about,
You let your guard down
And I took advantage

you wanted my all
Something I couldn't afford
To give at that time

Now we both moved on
I hope you forgive me

Don't Wait Til I Die to Love Me

I hope my actions didn't turn you
cold

I hope you learned from the mistake
that was me and grew from it.

The Flight

Once I decided
I needed a change
I stuffed my regrets
In a duffle bag
And booked a flight

There I was,
rushing through the airport
With the weight
of my burdens
Stressing my back and shoulders

"Bag's too heavy"

Tsa said.

I stood to the side
And discarded a few memories
I no longer needed

"Still too heavy"
Tsa said, again

More memories
More mistakes
Were tossed away
The bag was three times lighter

Don't Wait Til I Die to Love Me

So, I tried again

"Sorry sir, you can't get on with
this bag."
Tsa said

Running out of time,
I tossed the bag to the side
And sprinted to the flight gate

That's when I realized
It's impossible to move on,
It's impossible to grow
When you carry
regrets everywhere you go

I boarded the flight and never
looked back

Michael Tavon

Moonlight Kisses

I tend to get
jealous
when the moonlight
kisses your skin

My Crazy Mind

Last night
I broke down
Pillow soaked from my wet eyes,
Crying to the moon
Begging the lord to bring clarity
To this clouded mind
Searching for Answers,
I may never find,
Tears running fast
as if they're
Trying to cross the finish line

She called me via FaceTime
I was too ashamed
To show my face
"Baby what's wrong" she asked

Nothing I'm fine"
As I sobbed,
Trying to pick up
the scattered pieces
Of brain
"Baby talk to me"

More tears flow
My nose erupts
And I said
"What am I doing wrong?"

Michael Tavon

"I'm too young to be feeling this
old"
"What if my dreams never come
true?"
"I don't want us to end"

My mind was a loaded gun
And self-doubt
Were the silver bullets
Bursting from my mouth

She kept calm and caught
Every word in her palm
And said
"I promise, you don't have to
worry, everything is fine. You
don't have to cry; our love is
forever"

I wiped my face and smiled
Sometimes simple reassurance

Settles the chaos brewing
Inside an unstable mind

<u>Full Moon</u>

Watching the Full moon
With you, brings solace and warmth
when the dark clouds roar

Michael Tavon

New Life

From beautiful strangers

to intimate friends

Where pain ended,

happiness began

Don't Wait Til I Die to Love Me

Life of a Worker

Since age 15,
I've been putting
on a uniform
Clocking in
Taking orders,
Pulling freight
Rushing to eat during
30 minute breaks
Giving a thousand dollar effort
While getting paid minimum wage
A modern slave,
No benefits,
Too broke for vacations
I busted my ass
to receive 50 cent raises

Since age 15
17 workplaces
30 something managers
Twice the amount of supervisors
Late night shifts
that bled into the morning hours
Laboring with a fever
Because I couldn't call off

Working Since 15
I have nothing to

Show for but
A sprained knee
migraines
Pinched nerves in my back
And frostbite
Just for checks
That didn't make
a difference in my life
Since 15
I've quit
I've been fired
And laid off without reason
Because no matter

how hard I worked
I was always a disposable asset

Half of my life has been spent
On the clock
I've wasted
Holidays
Birthdays
And Special events
On places that didn't
give a shit about me

I'm tired to say the least
I'm tired and I just want to be
free

Viva La Vida

Life tested my will

Without giving me time to study

But I passed with good faith

Now I'm on to the next course

And I'm ready to take on

Any challenge with confidence.

Life and Death

My relationship with death
Has been much healthier lately
Fear no longer strikes
at the thought of my demise
Nor am I eager to meet it
I'm right in between
Which means,
The little things
Does not weigh a ton
On this light heart of mine
Like
Money
Popularity
Or
What people think of me
Does not matter in the slightest

I could die any day
and I'm fine with that.
why give a shit about
The things I can't take with me
When my body rests

Rumors die
Popularity fades
And Money gets buried in safes

But the memories I make
The smiles I create

Don't Wait Til I Die to Love Me

And the hearts I touch
Will last for eternity
That's what makes life

worth living
And death more liberating

Michael Tavon

Rainstorms

When the sound of rain
Plays through the open window
magic we create

When We Die

When we die
Do our souls
Wander aimlessly
To the moon
So they can
Shed light on the loved
Ones they left behind

Or do they
Party from body to body
Until they decide
to settle down
with the right one - again

When we die

Where do our souls go?
Do they embark on a never ending
Journey to fulfill their purpose
Or do they
Dwell, the surface
Feeling worthless

Where do our souls go?

Moonlight Lover

She can't help
but to get lost
in the moonlight
as it shines
through the window

Soul of Poets

We expose our naked souls

Hoping our words

will be heard

By people

Empathetic enough

To understand

Poets are the most fearless

humans on earth

Michael Tavon

Poet's Honor

I have

poetry flowing

Through my veins

Keeping my heart alive

Without these words

Embedded in my DNA

I would cease to exist

My life would have no meaning

Why Fear

People fear death
But there's far worse,
Like living to impress others,
Being confined behind bars
For a crime you didn't do,
never finding love,
Living without purpose,
Listening to the news
The list goes on and on

People fear death
Because the afterlife
Is unknown,
to a curious mind
the afterlife
Is just a new adventure

Michael Tavon

Lil' Wanderer

Travel through books
you will never
Feel lost

Stuck

Self-doubt and loathing
Are my best friends, I believe
They will never leave

Dear brain,

Why must you torture me
with memories
that's been buried deep
for so long
they've become relics,

Somehow you rediscover
these unwanted memories
after many years passed
what is your purpose
for bringing these moments
back to surface
What's to gain, what's to learn
from something
gone and done?

Why must you remind
me of the past?
I must ask,
please answer

Don't Wait Til I Die to Love Me

I am dying to know.

because some moments

I wish to not remember

Anymore

Eternal Love

Feels like
I've fallen in love
with your soul
a thousand times before,
And I will
A million times more

Unremember You

You didn't want my heart
for what it was
Making me feel
less than enough
You'd come into my bed
When it was dark
Then left before
the sun woke up
Too often I reached
for your touch
Then pull back with nothing
but air-filled palms
You were so calm
In the way you hurt me
Like giving pain
came natural to you

Now it's time to
Erase our memories
until your face becomes faint,

I'm resetting my brain

to the day before we met
so, I can successfully
Unremember you.

<u>With You</u>

Some say "less is more"

This explains why

It feels like the universe

Is In my arms

When I'm alone

With you

Farewell, Old me

Farewell,

to the old version of me

I didn't love you the way

you deserved to be

I hope you don't resent me,

I have grown

To appreciate myself,

Because of you

Goodbye Heartbreak

I wonder if heartbreak
Gets jealous at the sight
Of me parading around
with the love of my life
Does heartbreak regret
Letting me go
Since it sees
How much I've grown

I wonder if heartbreak
Wishes it never left
Me to mend the broken pieces
All by myself

Now heartbreak
Stares from a distance

Michael Tavon

Dreaming and wishing

For another chance
It won't get again

Magical is She

It's magical,
How she makes
sadness disappears
In the blink of an eye
With her smile
And witty lines,
She has the power
To humor a weary heart
On the darkest nights

Utopia

to think,
How much better the
world would be
If books and self-love
were advertised
As much as
fast food and alcohol

Love High

My eyes
are addicted to your smile
That's why I feel high
when I gaze at you

Michael Tavon

RIP MJ

"How could you miss a person you've
never met?"
Some may ask.

Well it's possible to miss
someone's soul more than their
presence.

Swallowed my Pride

My pride was the pill
I swallowed,
more than prescribed
Because My desire for you
to love me
Trumped my self-respect
"We're just friends"
you would say
While climbing into my bed,
My heart knew I deserved
more of you,
More than you,
But I would take a swig of water
So my pride could slide
Down my throat with ease,
Every time you'd stare deeply into
me
I knew we weren't meant to be
But I thought eventually
You'd want me
How I wanted you
If I proceeded
To give my heart to you
exclusively

Michael Tavon

Over time
I nearly overdosed
On my own pride
Then I realized chasing
After you was not worth
Losing my life

Drunk

Sometimes,
When you're drunk off pride
You do things you will regret
With a sober mind.

She's my Rock

On the nights
my mind spirals
into a hurricane of madness,
and self-doubt begins to
consume my sanity,
she calms the storm
with her powerful words of
encouragement

The Observer

I'm not an introvert, just
observant. I peep my surroundings
before letting my guard down. I
gotta be aware before I set my
energy free in any space. My
conscious must be clear in
unfamiliar territories. So, when
I'm silent amongst a crowd, it's
not because I'm shy, I'm feeling
out the vibes.

Michael Tavon

<u>Moon Moods</u>

Despite her many moods and hues
Mother nature does not apologize
for her raw emotions,
Neither should you.

Colors

I paint hopeful days
With new dreams and vivid hues
from yesterday's blues

Rebirth

I think of death
As liberation -
A fresh start
I'm in no rush
to start over
My soul loves
The body it's in now
But once this body expires
My soul is eager to begin
A new journey
In a new world
In a new time
Passing away
Is more liberating than life
I know it is
Because I've
Lived and died
Many times

<u>Jomo</u>
I am at a place
Where very few
have found themselves
It's where I've found
bliss without vanity
I do not lust for more women,
I do not thirst over
  new clothes or shoes
I have no desire to go to clubs
Or social events
The joy of missing out
Has led me to a haven
My heart can be free of
Yearning for things and places
That do not serve purpose in my lie

Michael Tavon

Goodnights

When the sound of rain plays

outside our window,

we cuddle so

warmly,

we melt into

each other.

Rhythm and Bliss

My fingertips dance

On the surface of her skin,

wild and carefree

As she sleeps so peacefully

They move and slide

from hips to thighs

To the symphony

of her heartbeat

Her body,

the perfect stage

For my hands to dance

In a blissful rhythm

Michael Tavon

Braveheart

With so much chaos and bullshit

going on in the world,

it's easy to turn off your

emotions, go numb.

The world needs love

Now more than ever

Promise to always

wear your heart

on a sleeve

no matter how cold

the weather gets.

<u>Lust for Life</u>

My passion for life

will never evaporate.

My heart is wild

my soul is free,

I have a lust for adventure

And a thirst for experience

For as long as I live

My beautiful mind

Will shine.

<u>Falling in</u>

I fall deeper in love when

I gaze into the depth of her

mesmerizing eyes

Moonsoulchild

Every day I thank her for loving me. Her existence will never be taken for granted. I shower her with reassurance, parade her with affection, and fill her lungs with laughter to ensure her day doesn't end in sadness. It's the simple things that makes a good woman happy. Love is not expensive, showing it is free.

Michael Tavon

The Frauds

it pisses me off how
the fucking frauds
Can manipulate their way
to first place
While the real artists struggle to
get the chance to race

To the Women Who Hurt Me

My heart no longer aches due to the pain you gave. I understand, you were afraid, your insecurities consumed you. I gave my all whenever you needed it, sadly it was never enough

Maybe I'm to blame as well. Maybe my downfall was falling for you too soon. Maybe, I should've soothed your trust issues with more consistency. Maybe I could have tried to harder. Maybe I should not have tried at all.

All in all, you made me feel inadequate, insignificant. For the nights you slept in my bed while dreaming of the man who hurt you. For the nights you fantasized about your ex while I was inside you. For the times you tap danced around the question "What are we?" I forgive you.

The heartache you gave does not
make you less of a good woman. I
promise. I just hope you've healed
from your past scars. I hope you've
found love within yourself. I hope
you've found the beautiful love
you've been running from your whole
life. If not, I know you will, and
I wish you well.

Trust Issues

Trust,
Such a fragile entity
That weighs a ton
We loan our trust to people
Hoping their shaky hands
Are strong enough to carry
the responsibility
Of never hurting us
While loving them
Unfortunately, by the time
we realize they can't
hold our trust
its purity is tainted
With cracks, scars, and permanent
fingerprints.

When someone new comes along
We hesitate to give
our damaged goods away.
Even though,
We still yearn to love
Our trust is too fucked up
To give away again.
We protect this trust
At all cost,
Refusing to allow another
Pair of hands to break it.

Michael Tavon

When someone gets too close
Our anxiety races a mile
A minute
Its proof, we never truly heal from
the past.

Cat and Mouse

I thought
Distanting myself
Would make you miss
me for a change
instead,
you fled into the arms
of another one.
joke's on me

A Letter to the Past me

 Dear you I'm sorry for how I abused you in ways your mind still can't fathom. You've come short so many times there should be a television show called, "A Thousand ways to disappoint yourself" in your honor. I hope that made you laugh, you always had a healthy sense of humor. Comedy is your favorite defense mechanism, when things get too intense for passive agressiveness. Anyways, remember how terrible you were at love? How you chased after anyone who gave you the time of day? How you rushed into love every chance you got? How heartache after heartache made you feel worthless? Remember the sleepless nights laying in the dark wondering why? Every night a million whys ran through your mind. Remember when you were depressed and didn't know it? Remember feeling like a loser? You did not care about yourself at all, empty sex, weed and alcohol abuse,not sleeping. lol

I'm sorry for bringing up the past just know it's all in good fun. No seriously, you can laugh because life is better now. You've found pure self-love, an abundant love, you're pursing your dreams. You inspire people daily. Life isn't perfect, but it's better than ever.

I'm here to remind you, you are enough. Stop drowning in self-doubt. Please be patient. Be kind to yourself. And stop worrying about what's ahead and love what you have now.

A Sad Love Story

He stares at the rain
As time passes
Hoping she'll comeback
So he can forgive the mistakes she
made, again
he stays because he fears moving on
and starting over
It's sad to see someone's mental
state wither away
Because his idea
of love is tainted
Thinking the more he tolerates her
shit
The stronger they'll become
One day I hope he realizes
his power,
I hope he lets go of the burden
holding him back
So he can rise above the madness.

Generational Trauma

Families with the most issues
Mock depression and treat therapy
like a punchline. Mental health is
never addressed. Instead of seeking
help, they try to fill their voids
with ounces of liquor. Drowning
their pain and sorrows by the swig.
They refuse to have healthy
conversations
They rather smile and gossip like
everything's fine
When they're breakingdown inside
These coping techniques passed down
by generations before them
And they'll pass it down to their
children
Creating a neverending chain
Of sadness.

Michael Tavon

Fuck Ice

No family deserves to be separated
by force and deported. Children
crying in cages like stray animals.
Facists have no shame they have
more respect for guns than people.
Their hearts are more evil than
equal. They treat women like
property and make jokes about the
ones starving in poverty. Their top
priority is the mighty dollar.
Making money at any cost, they
don't give a fuck about the lives
lost.

Deadbeat fathers

How could you plant
your seed in a womb
Then vanish after a beautiful life
blooms

Fucking coward ,
They're probably better off,
You don't deserve them
at all

I hope every dream
You have
Reminds you
how much of a bitch you are

I hope you never
feel good about yourself
A man who can't love his child Is a
man who doesn't deserve peace

Michael Tavon

Baggage Claim

Your baggage isn't too heavy, you
just have to find someone strong
enough to help you carry it.

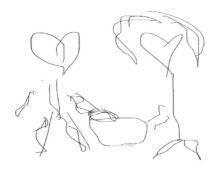

Self-Love and More

Being in love with
the right person
comes effortlessly
when the love you have for your
self as abundant as
clouds in the sky

Michael Tavon

The Key

Self- love requires
patience,
forgiveness,
and accountability
the three most difficult concepts
to grasp
when you're young
I've learned the longer
You hold grudges
the more bitter you become
We always want to
hold on to the pain
and refuse to move
away from the past
We hate to be wrong,
Convincing the mind
We're the victim
And nothing is ever our fault
We create this confort zone
And make it a home
Whilst begging for a change
And hoping for growth.

Simplicity

As I stare at the moon
from the deck of my apartment
Birds sing,
crickets chirp,
in perfect harmony
Under the stars,
A cool breeze ruffling
The leaves of the towering trees
Cars speed by on the highway,
The simplicities
Of the night
are worth living for
The music nature makes
Goes unappreciated,
Like most beautiful things
Our earth has to offer

Michael Tavon

Fatal Situationship

We just Fucked
And
Fucked
And
Fucked
Hoping one day
it would turn into love,
Every night
We bit our tongues
To hide our truest thoughts
While giving away
our most intimate parts,
And affection
Hoping it would manifest
Into something special
Instead,
We continued this act
Until one of us cracked
Voices were raised
Tears were shed
In the end
We never spoke again.

Don't Wait Til I Die II

Don't wait 'til
my heart stops pumping
to embrace me.

Don't wait 'til
my vision fades to prove
how much I mean to you.

Don't wait 'til
I can no longer hear to say
all the good things
you were too stubborn to say.

Please, I beg of you,
Don't wait 'til
I die to love me.
I need your love now,
more than ever.

Leaving the Dark

Even with the pressure

of her burdens

Weighing down on her shoulders

She continues to move forward

Taking small strides

Toward the sunlight

Slowly leaving

the darkness behind

She knows carrying her past

Will make her stronger

But the future will bring

Peace and clarity

So, giving up

Is not an option.

True Art

To be an artist is to constantly
flirt with adventure while making
love to new ideas

Ethereal Being

I may seem overprotective
of energy at first
But understand this
When I let down my guard
And my soul becomes comfortable
In your presence
You'll gain access to a world
too ethereal for common folk
I possess oceans of emotions,
most will drown in,
a mountain of thoughts
inside this beautiful mind,
And a heart so rare and pure
Scientists haven't discovered
anything like me before
See, my existence radiates
in dimensions
My smile alone
Will glare your eyes.
So are you ready,
To be exposed to a world
You quiet haven't seen before.
I must know before I let you in,
I can't allow another one
To hurt me, again
others weren't ready

Don't Wait Til I Die to Love Me

for me to begin with
I've learned my lesson.
So take your time to answer
There's no need to rush

Michael Tavon

<u>Be Free</u>
Let go of the weight
of your mistakes
so, you can fly
freely again

The Past Ghost

The past,
Is a ghost that haunts us all
No matter how fast you run
It will be there
Looming, over your shoulder
The more you try to deny
The more it will remind you
Of your mistakes
Your pain
Your traumas
And drama
But once you accept
The past
With dignity
You become stronger
and wiser
as the image slowly fades
and the memories grow distant
your present becomes easier
and the future gets brighter
The ghost will disappear
When fear is nonexistent

Michael Tavon

Love YOU

It's human nature

To want to fit in,

Gain acceptance from peers

We all want friends

We all want love

At what cost?

Are you willing to dull

your personality

To fit in with the wrong crowd

Or would you rather

Shine as yourself and standout?

Should you comprise your character

To fit the mold of society's

standards

Or be you fearlessly

And fuck who chooses

Don't Wait Til I Die to Love Me

to misunderstand you

These questions are rhetorical

You should already know the

answers.

Always remember,

Keeping up a façade

more is stressful than

Being yourself

Michael Tavon

Bliss

Bliss has a home,
it resides inside me.

Say Goodbye
Say goodbye to the people
Who use your insecurities
To manipulate you
To get what they want

Say goodbye to the people
Who dangle your past
Over your head
When you're outgrowing
The lifestyle you once lived

Say goodbye to the people who
Find it hard to accept
Your decision to choose
What's best for you

Say goodbye to the people
Who only love you
When it's convenient for them

Say goodbye
To the people who
Don't feed your dreams
With support and praise
It's time to let go
Of the people who aren't
Hitting your soul with light,

Michael Tavon

watering your heart with love
And planting seeds of hope
In your mind.

Deep Sea Dive

Falling in love
with the wrong person
is like deep sea diving
Without equipment
You fall so deeply
into this boundless territory
Wide eyed, filled with hope
Adrenaline rushes through
Your limbs and spine
As you wander aimlessly.
The deeper you swim,
the darker the surroundings,
The colder the currents
the surface becomes
More distant.
Suddenly, adrenaline turns to
anxiety
Your breath runs short
You realize
You were unprepared to embark
On this wild adventure
You find yourself alone
And vulnerable,
With your feet
rock bottom
For a while you sulk
Wondering if there's
anywhere to go

Michael Tavon

Then you begin to swim
Towards the sliver of light
Peeking through the dark
You're tired but resilient
You refuse to quit
At last you emerge
from the water
Fresh air hits your skin
And fills your lungs
You saved yourself
And learned a valuable lesson
Never take air for granted
Even when you're falling in love

Parting Ways

These tears don't fall for anyone
But they fell for you
As they drizzle from my iris
To the surface of my skin
My vision of you gets blurry
The apologies I expect to hear
from your pride filled mouth
Are held hostage
by the back of your tongue
I begin to doubt our love
Or whatever it was
You stand, shoulders slumped
As if you don't comprehend
The damage you caused
And how hard
it's for me to let go.
I was attached to the idea
Of you and I finding forever
Along the way we
Lost ourselves,
parted ways
Came back around,
tried again
We must admit
Our journey together must end
It's hard to say goodbye

Michael Tavon

to a friend
But the purpose has been met
My mind understands,
These tears only fell
Because my heart still can't fathom
You being far away

Biggest Fan

My heart celebrates
your existence,
The biggest fan in the stance
Cheering loud and proud
During the ups and downs
My heart pumps
The colors you exude

Beautiful Blur

Life is a beautiful blur
Filled with vague memories
Of a thousand yesterdays
And visions of tomorrow's
Not guaranteed

We rush to the days
too far ahead
And run for the moments
we will never capture again

If only we live at the speed
Of which we are meant
We'd enjoy the beauty of the
present

Instead, we prefer
To live a big
beautiful blur

Home

My heart never felt
lost with you,
Since the beginning
Your love felt like home

The Highest Feeling

Your love is too good
to be true
I rub my eyes when
I look at you
To ensure you're no mirage,
Or a figment living in my
imagination
Pinch me
Hope I'm not dreaming
See, real love is surreal
how something so magical
Can be this real
You're the greatest experience
My heart has felt
Our love will burn forever
My flame
Won't last for anyone else

Inner Child

Time flies
when your inner child dies
So, set it free, outside
Allow its imagination
To run wild
To keep it alive

Don't allow that child
To grow bitter in the dark
It will forever feel lost
With a void in its heart

Protect the child in you
Never let it get stolen
By heartbreak, jobs, death
Or self-loathing

Love the child inside you
Please don't neglect,
If it dies unloved
Your soul will be consumed
With regret

For the mistreated and misunderstood

I know the world can be a cruel
place
To open up to. Putting your truth
on full display for the world to
see is scary as hell. Being
different is rejected more than
respected, so you conceal being
yourself to protect your mental
health. It hurts, putting on a
mask, pretending to fit in to make
others comfortable. All the while
your soul is crying inside, the
truth dying to burst free. I know
it's hard, but please free your
yourself before your soul burns to
dust. Fuck everyone who won't
accept you. There are people who
will love and protect you at all
cost. If you live with a heart
abundant with love and sincerity,
you'll find more clarity. Giving
more space for your supporters to
cheer for you on. To the people who
may judge, don't worry about them,

Don't Wait Til I Die to Love Me

they hate to see anyone happy in
their own skin, because they're not
brave enough to be who they truly
are.

Paracosm

When you over-fantasize about a
love you create the illusion of a
perfect relationship. You see past
the red flags and refuse to accept
their flaws. You neglect to soak in
their presence in the present
because you've drowned your mind in
a future that doesn't exist.
Sometimes, it's not your lover's
fault when your heart gets broken.
You made this person out to be
someone they never portrayed to be.
You turned blind when they showed
glimpses of their true selves. When
you want love so bad you rush into
situations that were supposed to
take time. Before you break your
heart again, remember to bask in
the present, develop a real raw
connection and not a fantasy.

The Notebook II

I pray
you and I
grow old
together
I refuse to
lose you
While we're
young
A love like
yours will be
impossible
To encounter
twice in one
lifetime

Money Problems

I have a toxic relationship
with money
It comes and goes
as it pleases
I'm happy when it's here
Miserable when it leaves
Then I feel worthless without it
I give it too much power
Maybe I should
Fall back for a while
Let it come to me,
Maybe it will stay this time
Maybe we should remain
Friends with benefits
Better yet,
I should value myself more
Stop giving into the allure
Of not being alone,
I no longer want to be
A slave to money
My mental health is more important

Sticks and Stones

Sticks and stones may break my
bones, but lies may leave scars
that last forever

Soul Searchin'

My soul wandered far beyond its
comfort zone to find the peace it
was searching for.

Anxiety II

I'm not the strongest fighter
But every night I find myself
Shadow boxing
With my anxiety
I jab away
Until my arms swell,
My persistence comes to no avail
As anxiety stands unfazed.

Its long reach and power
makes his punches impossible
to dodge,
A swift shot to my confidence
Makes my knees buckle
As I struggle to stay up
A right hook hits my mental health
and
Knocks me down,
And out for the count

Anxiety always wins
Because it knows my weakness

Michael Tavon

(My mind)
I think it's time to develop
A new strategy
I'm tired of losing to myself

Homecoming

What if god sends all its good
children home too soon because
earth doesn't deserve to have them
for too long?

Michael Tavon

Flourished

After the rainstorm
We flourished from the soil
And rose high in love

Vulnerable Soul

The idea of
being vulnerable
With your heart, body,
and soul
With someone new
Is scary,
After years of heartbreak
And giving your secrets
and deepest feelings
To old lovers
Who weren't strong enough
To carry the weight
Makes falling in love Again
seem daunting
It's hard to fathom
having pillow talk
At 3am with someone else,
Between all the
memories Created
Time spent,
And laughs shared
You thought the 'I love yous'
Would last forever
Then it all
came crashing down
Before you got
the chance to say goodbye,
You'd rather be alone

Michael Tavon

than to experience love
with a new soul
This is why
Moving on takes courage
But starting over
takes strength

The Flames

Think of a broken heart

As flames combusting

Across a beautiful forest

Limbs fall and break,

Leaves

burn to ashes

The plants of many hues

become smoke and grey

Mass destruction widespread

across the plain,

Until the life within

Becomes nonexistent,

Once the smoke clears

And the ashes blow away

The healing process begins,

Through the devastation

The soil became richer,

Michael Tavon

Roots became stronger,

over time

New plants emerge from the surface

More resilient than before

See, heartbreak may seem

Impossible to recover

from in the moment

But just like a burning Forrest

You will rise from the ashes

Stronger than ever before

If you give yourself time

Guard Up

I barricade
the doors and windows
When depression approaches
the doorstep
Its presence is no longer
Welcomed in my home

Michael Tavon

Body Telepathy

When your body speaks, I listen and
give in to her sensual wisdom, I'm
infatuated by the story she tells.

<u>Love.</u>

The 4 letter word nothing can be so
shallow yet so deep
How could something so bitter taste
this sweet?
Ever so common it is, yet rather
unique
It can make you weak like a hammer
to the knees
Yet makes you feel like you're
standing ten feet high
No drug, but it can be addictive,
Inflicted, by the cuts it leaves on
ya wrist kid
Are you willing to risk it?
I'm just metaphorically speaking
About the euphoria that it brings
to you for her,
Such a happy place
it can take you
Yet that same place
can break you
Into shells til
you no longer see yourself
In that broken mirror of trust
First, it's a crush then lust
Then becomes full grown

Michael Tavon

It's true, love makes you feel
young or steal your youth
til you're old and alone
Or with your happily ever after
How could something worth a
thousand tears
Give you so much laughter you wake
up every morning after
Pleased that you have her
You grab her like your own it
Love is over time, but you fall in
the moment,
moments that can
last a lifetime
it can age like milk
or fine wine
Either way love is one of a kind

Love Language

It's the little kind gestures that
drives the heart wild

Michael Tavon

The Key

See, the key to love is finding
someone who doesn't pin down your
wings, with their ego and
insecurities, as you ascend to a
higher self. A relationship is
about contributing to your lover's
success without petty competition.
Your lover should push you towards
growth, not hold you back from it.
True love is about helping each
other reach the sky without
worrying about who does it first.

Late Night Feels

I sigh
at the thought of
not being good enough
My eyes
On the verge of pouring
My heart pounds heavily
I'm losing my balance
I can't rest
I can't think straight
With self-doubt
Clouding my mind

Michael Tavon

Emotional prison.

Your pain turns into rage,
When you slap shackles
on your emotions
and lock them in a cage

Set your feelings free
Give them the ability
To find inner peace

When you imprison your feelings
You become empty, listless
— Dying for a healing
In a hopeless place
You'll forever try to escape
Alone, crying for a warm embrace

So breakdown
When you're falling fast
misery won't last
After the storm passes

Every day, Love

Nothing in this life
Will break my spirit
As long as my days
End and begin with you

Michael Tavon

Addicted to Numbness

I've seen many of my peers
Turn into zombies over the years
Some swallow pills
to escape their fears

Some shoot ice
through their Veins
to numb the pain
Until their soul drains
Then sleep the day away

Others, drink until
Their memories fade
As hours turn into days
Their demons become friends

So many of my peer
Give up before giving
themselves a chance
Maybe the pain
is too deep to withstand

Maybe, they think being

Don't Wait Til I Die to Love Me

Numb is better than feeling
Maybe they think a
slow death
is better than Healing

Michael Tavon

Please Stay Alive

Deep down inside
There's still a beautiful soul in
there
I wish you would learn how to
forgive yourself
And the ones who abused your heart
So you can rise from the ashes and
rubble
Your mind is filled with so
much internal struggle
you turn to vices
To help negate the pain,
as a friend who cares
I beg of you to
Discard the pills,
Throw away the blade,
Toss the syringes
Avoid empty sex
You're not weak for *being* broken,

Or feeling hopeless

Don't Wait Til I Die to Love Me

there are better ways to cope
Stop dwelling in the darkness
There's still some light left in
you

In Hiding

Sometimes, hiding
from my problems
feels more comforting
than confronting them

The Unwritten

There are still many
Unwritten chapters
in your story
don't be in a rush
to end it here
The longer you live
The stronger your
character becomes
write through the blocks,
you will overcome,
the greatest stories
are told by wise minds
and broken souls

A Poem for The Homeless

I wanna do more than
Give spare change
I wanna help bring
Your life real change
Despite the mistakes
you've made you deserve
a second chance
It hurts my heart to see you
digging through trash cans
Or curled under a tree
when it rains
I often wonder
Where do you go
when it snows.
Even though
The world has given up on you,
and you've given up on yourself,
I wish had the resources to help
No way in hell
Anyone should be flying private
jets
Wearing thousand dollar clothes
Living in a home of 12 bedrooms
With a family a four,
as you suffer alone
Something needs to change
Something has to be done
The world ain't fair
You deserve more

Don't Wait Til I Die to Love Me

Michael Tavon

Ghostin

I vanished to see what it feels
like to be missed.

Algedonic

My heart was addicted to pain
because it kept beating for you
Trapped in the cycle
Of forgiving your careless ways
Knowing you would never change
I ran to the sun and back
To make you stay,
My eyes were too blind to see
your love was just a mirage
I created in my mind,
Because I was afraid of the reality
of sleeping alone,
The more you shook me off
The more I latched onto you
I admit, it was my fault
I allowed you to seduce me
With empty promises
I was dumb when it came to love
But I'm no longer a novice
Thanks to you

Life is Precious II

People waste so much

Precious time

Complaining about

What they want

What they have

And what they can't change

Instead,

of looking to the sky

And admiring the silver lining

In each cloud,

Or inhaling fresh air

During a calm walk

through the park,

As sunlight

Kisses their skin

Don't Wait Til I Die to Love Me

a thousand times,

Or counting the stars

While sipping mint tea,

Some people don't take the time

To appreciate the universe for

constantly reminding them----

"You're still here"

"You're still are loved"

"You're not alone"

Because they're too focused on

Chasing material pleasure

and not adventure.

Temporary Forever

As difficult as it was
I had to let you out of sight,
Out of mind,
Out of my dreams
To set myself free
From the beautiful mess
we created
Why keep trying to revive
Something that's been dying
Long before we put our pride
to the side
It's too late, now
But let's take some time
To appreciate the moments
that were filled with
fire and lust
Before the trust got fucked up
Between us
Let's thank each other for
The pleasant memories
And unforgettable love we made,
We were both
Lessons and blessings
To each other
Although the promise
of being together forever
Was broken
The love we shared
in this lifetime
Is something worth treasuring

Don't Wait Til I Die to Love Me

But we can't hold onto the past
If we're not presently serving
purpose
To our hearts

I'd much rather leave
While I can appreciate
The good times we shared
Than to break my heart
Trying to fix something
that will never be again

Survival

You cry because
you loved hard
You cry for
the effort you put in
you cry for all the time
will never get back
it's okay to shed tears
Allow yourself to heal
By shedding the pain
one tear at a time
don't be consumed
by the love you lost
Wipe the wetness
from your eyes and
Celebrate the strength you acquired
After surviving a broken heart

Believe in Magic

She's grown so accustom
to men performing disappearing acts
after filling her ears
with sweet nothings
and empty promises
That when a good man appeared
from thin air
she doubted his integrity
and questioned his intentions
He attempted to change her mind
He tried to make her believe
in magic again
but to no avail her failed
and like the men before her
He vanished too
til this day
She shuts her eyes tight
Whenever she sees magic
even when its real.

Michael Tavon

Guidance

She pours her soul into
Every glass half empty
To inspire the world around her
It's easy to gravitate towards
A magnetic spirit like hers, such
A blessing to be in her presence
And learn from her guidance

Always Care

Do you ever feel like you're
running out of tears to shed?
Like your heart is running low on
compassion?
Are you starting to feel numb to
tragedy

I know caring for
this fucked up world gets
exhausting, but someone must do it

Michael Tavon

The Garden

When done right, love is a
continuous ascension to a higher
self. As the years pass, you plant
seeds of devotion and compassion
into the soil of your trust and
your relationship will flourish,
and blossom into a vibrant flower,
with a stem impossible to break.
Stay strong through the storms and
trust each other through the trying
times. Always be vulnerable and
communicate with empathy. Love
can't be watered with ego or pride,
put those to side, so you two can
live a long prosperous fulfilling
love. The most beautiful
relationships don't dwell in
darkness, because they only grow in
the light.

(For Andy and Liz)

Rising From

When you're shrouded by
Smoke and embers
From the fire life caused,
It may seem impossible to survive
It may seem impossible
to find the breath of fresh air
you're desperately gasping for,
if you trudge
through the flames,
with hope and fearlessness,
and your head held high
you will arise from the ashes
despite getting burned
no flame is strong enough
to kill you, believe in yourself
even after you break down
or have a slight moment of weakness
please keep rising
until you find the peace and love
Waiting for you on the other side.

(For Laura)

Michael Tavon

<u>Dear You</u>

The one my heart explodes

in supernovas for

You brighten my sky

with your crescent smile.

Your laughter brings peace

to this uneasy soul.

As complex as life gets

The simplicities of your existence

Makes it all worth while

The stars in your eyes

Ignites the small part of darkness

That dwells inside me

Without you,

My space feels empty,

Your heart is so vast

I gotta share you

With the world

Don't Wait Til I Die to Love Me

Because your love is infinite

And your heart is filled

With galaxies of passion

That's why I'm infatuated

by your aura

it draws me in like gravity

Michael Tavon

Selflessness

It doesn't hurt to give love
To those who need it
So please don't be stingy
Give as much as you can
When you can.

Your Road to Self

Watching you grow into
This magnificent woman
Who inspires me to be
a better person everyday
Has been a sensational ride
Filled with up and bumps,
before, we embarked
on this journey
you told me to buckle up
because life gets wild,
you wanted me to be safe
in case the roads got rocky

As your passenger
I let you lead us
To your destination
While providing guidance
on the days you felt lost,
I thank you for trusting me

We traveled so far together
And I got to witness
you make it to
your beautiful destination,
You beautiful human

Michael Tavon

You had the courage
To follow your dreams
Now you're a woman
With miles of joy ahead of her

Thank you for allowing me
to join the ride

Insomnia or Not

Late night thoughts
are my worst enemy,
When my drowsy eyes beg
For sleep
I count sheep
Breathe,
Meditate,
Toss and turn
Somehow
I end up with my eyes
piercing through the darkness,
I wonder why am I still here?
How many people really care?
A thousand thoughts race
through my mind,
In a flash,
Memories from the present
Future and past,
Occur
I question my mistakes
And wonder where would
I be without them
Or the love of my life
I think what if
I never did this or if I really did

that,
What would happen
if I turned back the hands of time,
Scrap the past,
Start from scratch
My mind tries to travel
through time
That's why
The things I can't control,
controls my thoughts the most
I know
I don't have insomnia
my mind just loves to run wild past
midnight

<u>Epiphany</u>

It took me a while to realize
I wasn't in love. I was obsessed
with the idea of not being alone
anymore, that's why I dealt with
the pain they caused for so long,

Michael Tavon

I Hope, I Pray

I pray my purpose is served
Before I leave this earth

I hope to
inspire more love than hate
Before my soul withers away

I pray my words
plant seeds of hope
To harvest change
for brighter days

I hope my efforts
don't go in vain
I pray earth becomes
a better place
After my final days

Dying Mother

Earth is crying for love
Her children been
neglecting her for too long,
We watch her burn,
from the core
People seem to care more
About money and taxes
What about the trees?
What about the dying animal
families?
What about the air?
What about the oceans?
Mother Earth is
running out of breath
She's gasping for air
Can we come together
To save our mother
because we're nothing without her

Michael Tavon

Talk it Out

We've come too far to let
a disagreement break us apart
Let's sit down, talk it out
Hear each other out

Your point of view
is as valid as mine,
let's take the time
To understand each other's mind

There's no need to yell,
Fight, or cry. We're mature enough
to find a solution
Without causing pain

Journey 2 You

Don't fear the pitch black
Road ahead,
You may feel lost
In the start
But the journey to self-discovery
requires traveling through darkness
To discover the light
you're desperately seeking for,
Use the stars as your guide
Pay attention to the signs
The universe provides,
you'll find the light
I promise,
Be brave,
Travel fearlessly
Embrace the road
that was paved for you
You'll make it through

Michael Tavon

The Truth is

Some people choose to overlook you
Or devalue your gifts
for reasons unknown
no matter how much energy you
expand
trying to prove why they should
appreciate you
they continue to treat you like an
afterthought, I guess,
One of the most difficult things
about life is accepting the fact
some won't appreciate you until you
die or walk away.

Fear and Loathing II
Heart buried in emotions
Palm soaked in tears
Yearning for the days
Far from here

Anxiety strikes through
my veins like lightening
Today I'm content,
But the future is frightening

Working up my nerves
Over something I can't control
I should listen to some music
Or take a stroll

The future I dread
But I'm eager to see
If I'll grow into everything
I strive to be

As fear runs through my bones
Nothing is more intimidating
than the unknown

Michael Tavon

Broken Home Syndrome

You fail at love
Over and over
Because you learned how to love
From a broken home.

<u>Driving Anxiety</u>

Sometimes,
when I gaze out the window
of the passenger side
I wonder why
I can't be like those
Who are comfortable
Driving between the lines

I'm cursed with the anxiety
That fills my body with fear
When I'm behind the wheel

My confidence
goes out the door
The moment I hit the road
My led toe,
Pedal to the floor

I drift lane to lane
Because streets feel so narrow
Don't know where to go
Can't follow the arrows

Michael Tavon

My vision gets blurry,
When I feel worried
About drivers behind
Honking me to hurry

I wish I could be normal
I wish this could be fixed
Because being an adult
With driving anxiety
feels like shit

Moving Forward II

You've convinced yourself
That life is worthless
without this one person
the same person who was a stranger
the day before you met them,
there was a time
life was fine
before you
knew of their existence,
so why give them
the power to cripple
your spirit now?

Remember who you were before,
but never forget the heartache
You feel today,
You will become an unbreakable
Force, moving forward

Michael Tavon

Dear Lord

Please give me a sign
Guide me to the light
I want to know if doing right

Give some indication,
is this dream worth chasing
Or if it's time I'm wasting?

My mind clouded with rage
I'm praying for changed
Will there be brighter days?

Please, Let know me know
Do I have reason to hope
Or will my dreams fester in snow?

A Letter to God

Hey, it's me your distant child, I
know we haven't spoke in a while,
but tonight I'm reaching out;
hoping you'll listen. In the past
I've tried to be independent,
navigate without your guidance, now
I submit; I'll listen to your
wisdom
Speak to me, provide the clarity I
am seeking. You know I don't ask
for much that's why I get down when
I don't get what I want or what I
believe I deserve. I'm still
learning how to trust your time
more than mine. I struggle with
patience, because I'm eager to see
what the future holds. I bet you
get a kick out of me trying to
force things to go in my favor. I
know you laugh and say 'I told you
so' when you see me stumble over
the same mistake over and over. I
know you love me; I know you won't
ever give up on me. Just give me
some clarity. Help me see what I
am missing. Give me the mental
space to think straight. I need

some confirmation, tell me I'm
doing right, tell me this is my
purpose. Give some indication that
I'm running in the right direction.

Sincerely, me

Fin.

Michael Tavon

Connect:

Twitter: @BymichaelTavon
Instagram: @ByMichaeltavon
Facebook: Michael Tavon

Cover Art Illustrator

Intagram: @Woe89s
Twitter: @Woe89s

Twitter: @Moonssoulchild
Facebook: Moonsoulchild
Instagram: @Moonsoulchild

Other Books by Michael Tavon

Novels:

God is a Woman
Far from Heaven

Poetry Collections:

Young Heart, Old Soul
Nirvana: Pieces of Self-Healing Vol 1 & 2
A Day Without Sun
Songs for Each Mood

Michael Tavon

Made in the USA
Monee, IL
24 January 2021